Saptashloki

The Seven Verses from Devi Mahatmyam

Transliteration, Translation and commentary
-k.koushik

First Printing, 2017

ISBN-13: 978-1543048216

ISBN-10: 1543048218

Printed in the United States of America

Contents

ABOUT THE HYMN 1

POORVA PEETIKAA 3

NYAASA 14

SHLOKA 1 16

SHLOKA 2 22

SHLOKA 3 29

SHLOKA 4 35

SHLOKA 5 39

SHLOKA 6 43

SHLOKA 7 47

DURGAA SAPTASHLOKEE IN DEVANAGARI SCRIPT 52

DURGAA SAPTASHLOKEE IN ENGLISH SCRIPT 54

About the Hymn

Durgaa saptashatee which is also known as Devi Maahaathmyam or Chandi paatha or Durgaa paatha is one of the most powerful hymns for the worship of mother Durgaa. (Mother Shakti - the embodiment of all power) The hymn is a part of Maarkandeya Puraana and the hymn is called Durga Saptashatee for it is comprised of seven hundred mantras praising the mother goddess and describing her great deeds. Each mantra in it is very sacred and powerful and is praised in the Tantras and mantra shaastras. The goddess is worshipped in three main forms Mahaakaali (the controller and embodiment of time) Mahaalakshmi (the controller and embodiment of all wealth) and Mahaasaraswati (the controller and embodiment of all wisdom) through this sacred hymn.

For the ease of the devotees who cannot chant the seven hundred verses of the Devi Maahaathmya daily, our kind mother goddess instructed to chant the seven most important verses from the text. The collection of those seven shlokas is called Durgaa Saptashlokee.

In this book I will explain the meaning of those seven shlokas according to the commentaries of great Shaakta scholars (devotees of mother goddess) like Bhaaskara raaya maakhin, Naagoji bhatta and other scholars of the Shaakta tradition.

Each of the seven shlokas praise the goddess Durgaa and pray to her for different fruits. All of these verses are found in different chapters of the Devi Maahaathmya. Each of these shlokas is a mantra which can also be chanted separately to please the mother and to attain a particular benefit (fruit), pray for protection, wealth, good fortune and the mother's (Ambaa's) grace.

This hymn starts with a conversation between lord Shiva and Devi.

One who chants this hymn with true devotion for goddess Durgaa shall be blessed with all fortunes of life and will also attain self realization by the grace of the goddess.

Poorva peetikaa

शिव उवाच
देवि त्वं भक्तसुलभे सर्वकार्यविधायिनी ।
कलौ हि कार्यसिद्ध्यर्थमुपायं ब्रूहि यत्नतः ॥

śiva uvāca
devi tvaṃ bhaktasulabhe sarvakāryavidhāyinī
kalau hi kāryasiddhyarthamupāyaṃ brūhi yatnataḥ

Lord Shiva said

O Devi! you are easily attainable and approachable by your true devotees and you are capable of accomplishing everything for them. Please tell me a way to attain fulfillment and positive result in everything even in the era of kali.

Lord Shiva starts talking to the goddess.

He addresses her by the name Devi. The word Devi means goddess in general. It also means one who is luminous and bright. Devi also means one who does everything as a play. Her play is the five great deeds (panchakrutya) she is the Shakti (power) capable of doing panchakrutya.

The next word lord uses to address Devi is bhakta sulabhe - you are easily approachable and attainable by your true devotees, the connection between the name Devi and bhakta sulabhe is that, though you are the greatest goddess and you are high above everything, you answer your devotee's call because you are their loving mother. In whatever high position a mother may be seated in, she is always easily approachable by her dear children. Goddess being limitless, independent and free, she is not bound by anyone but she answers her devotees and blesses them, out of unconditional love and her natural motherhood.

Sarvakaaryavidhaayini - One who fixes all the tasks which are messed up. One who rectifies the troubles and hurdles and one who helps us do all the tasks by residing inside us in the form of powers, capabilities, strength and skills. The reason for using this name to refer Devi is because she is the one who helps us do the tasks and attaining desires through actions and hence she alone can and should instruct us with a way for fulfillment of all kinds of desires and hence lord Shiva is asking her to do so.

The lord refers to the kali era and asks for a method for accomplishing all desired tasks and attaining different kinds of fruits and benefits.

The lord particularly refers to the era of kali because, in kali era all the methods which are already prescribed by Vedas and Shaastras becomes nearly impossible to be followed perfectly.

Vedas prescribe Yagyas - sacred sacrifice rituals for attaining various benefits but the things that are to be offered through the Yagyas have lost their purity due to various reasons and pronouncing the Vedic mantras with the correct svara (Vedic tone) with pure mind and body has become very tough in the era of kali.

Pooja (worship by offering sixteen kinds of services to gods) done is also not perfect due to impurity in goods, lack of knowledge of rituals etc.

The path of Yoga recommends Dhyaana for the attainment of various fruits but doing Dhyaana with the optimum level of concentration and control of mind is also really hard as minds of the people of kali era are always wavering and easily distracted.

Different vows and austerities which are advised by the Smruthis and Puraanas are also hard to follow as the people of kali era are weak minded and also physically weak. Completing a simple fast with pure mind and devotion towards the deity following the rules etc are also very hard because people don't have mind control. So even if one fasts, thoughts of food wavers in mind and not thoughts of god.

Then there is no need for a discussion about long penances (tapas) which have been done by great seers (Rishis) in the past. We all know it's nearly impossible.

When the above mentioned methods are not done correctly by following the instructions thoroughly, the deed doesn't yield the expected fruits, there are also chances of adverse effects if the Krathu or Kriya (sacred deeds) is done without Shraddha. (faith and trust in the words of Vedas and Puraanas (i.e.) trusting the words mentioned and following it correctly and carefully.)

So lord Shiva is asking Devi to tell him a way through which all kinds of benefits can be attained easily. Lord praises the quality of Devi being easy with her devotees by calling her bhakta sulabhe. Which is completely true and hence lord Shiva expects Devi to reveal him the easy way for attaining desires for the benefit of her devotees.

Why does lord Shiva ask Devi about this? Lord Shiva is the almighty god who is the all knower.

(sarvagya)

Yes. Lord Shiva knows everything but he asks this to Devi for the benefit of the worlds. Though he is all knowing, he wants this method to be given to us through our kind mother goddess.

Shiva - the husband of Devi, enjoys listening to her greatness and glory in her own words This is also done to increase the trust of the devotees in this hymn. It is natural for the devotee to trust this hymn for it is given by the mother goddess and hence she will definitely be pleased when the hymn is chanted with devotion.

This shows us the kindness of lord Shiva and mother Devi for us beings. we are the ones who actually need a way to please her and she is always pleased by lord Shiva and he has no need to please her with a way of worship nor does he have a desire which has to be accomplished. The lord asks about this to Devi only out of his unconditional kindness and pity for us (his children)

Lord Shiva being our god and also our guru (Spiritual master), gives us a mantra to please the mother goddess.

The word yatnatah means by putting efforts. Here we should think. She is Devi and Devi means the one who does everything effortlessly and playfully. Then, why does the lord ask her to reveal a sacred way to please her by putting efforts.

Here the word putting efforts doesn't literally mean putting efforts. The meaning which the word gives out here is 'somehow' (i.e.) tell it somehow (in one way or the other, by some means) even though it is a precious secret.

Here the word yatna refers to the change in decision from not revealing the secret to revealing the secret. He rightly says that she has to put the effort in changing her mind to reveal this because it has never been revealed before and now the lord is asking Devi to reveal this hymn as there is no other method through which devotees could fulfill their wishes without any hardships.

Here we should understand that lord Shiva has no secrets which have to be opened to him, he being the all knower. The word 'tell' indicates that the way should be revealed to the world and so she should tell it somehow for the welfare of the beings though the method is precious and should not be generally given out.

देव्युवाच
शृणु देव प्रवक्ष्यामि कलौ सर्वेष्टसाधनम् ।
मया तवैव स्नेहेनाप्यम्बास्तुतिः प्रकाश्यते ॥

devyuvāca
śṛṇu deva pravakṣyāmi kalau sarveṣṭasādhanam
mayā tavaiva snehenāpyambāstutiḥ prakāśyate

shrunu - listen to me

deva - lord

pravakshyaami - I will tell you

kalau sarveshta saadhanam - a method for attaining all desires in kali era.

Mayaa - by me

Tava eva snehena - only because of love and affection to you, only because of your love and affection to me

Api - also (even the - in this context)

Ambaa stutih - hymn of Ambaa (mother goddess)

Prakaashyate - is revealed

Devi says

O lord, please listen to me, I will tell to you a way by which one can attain all that is desired even in the age of kali. This hymn of Ambaa is opened (revealed) to you by me only out of my love and affection for you.

Devi addresses lord Shiva as Deva.

The word Deva means god in general. It also means one who is luminous and bright. Deva also means one who does everything as a play. His play is the five great deeds (panchakrutya) (he does the five deeds with his power (Shakti - mother goddess)

Deva also means lord.

This name is praised in the Vedas

ये देवा देवा दिविषद: स्थ तेभ्यो वो देवा देवेभ्यो नम:
yē dēvā dēvā diviṣada: stha tēbhyō vō dēvā dēvēbhyō nama:

Deva and Devi has the same meaning, Deva is masculine and Devi is feminine.

This name shows that lord Shiva and Devi are non-different.

She asks the lord to listen. (shrunu) This word is an attention grabber used to indicate that you should listen attentively and something very important is going to be revealed or taught.

Pravakshyaami - I will tell you. The use of future tense here is to stress the point that this hymn was never revealed before.

Kalau sarveshta saadhanam - a way through which all kinds of desires can be fulfilled (even) in the age of kali.

We have already discussed why other methods don't give expected results in kali yuga. Devi says that the method which she is going to reveal now will yield all desired results even in kali era.

This method doesn't depend on the purity of goods and it doesn't have tough rules of austerity and penance. Doesn't require any special knowledge. Just by praising the mother through this hymn with devotion, desired benefits are bestowed. It is not tough like the Dhyaana maarga which requires single pointed concentration. Just by chanting the hymn with devotion even when the mind is wavering, the chanting of the hymn gradually gives you balance and stillness in mind.

By praising the goddess with this hymn, you understand the goddess and your love and devotion in her increases and the level of concentration increases with it.

Then Devi says that she is revealing this great secret hymn of Ambaa only out of her love and affection for lord Shiva.

The word 'api' generally means also. In this context the word 'api' means 'even the' and the word is used to express the importance of the hymn.

In this shloka, api ambaa stutih prakaashyate means even the ambaa stuti is reveled to you.

The word 'even' is used to express the preciousness of the hymn and the level of love and affection Devi has for the lord.

Devi says O lord, I Am revealing you even the ambaa stuti. (which I would never reveal at all) I am changing my mind only out of uncontrollable love to you. This tells us that Devi would do anything for lord Shiva.

Tavaiva snehena also means only because of your true love to me.. (i.e.) I am revealing this hymn only because I am pleased by your true love and affection.

The happy life of the children depends on parents' true love for each other and their children. Our parents lord Shiva and Shakti's love is the prime reason of our well being and hence the reason of revealing this hymn for our welfare is also their divine love.

Ambaa means mother. This hymn praises the mother goddess who is kind by nature and kindly guides us, purifies us and grants all our wishes without expecting us to put hard tedious efforts.

Nyaasa

ॐ अस्य श्रीदुर्गासप्तश्लोकीस्तोत्रमहामन्त्रस्य

नारायण ऋषिः ।

अनुष्टुभादीनि छन्दांसि ।

श्रीमहाकालीमहालक्ष्मीमहासरस्वत्यो देवताः ।

श्रीदूर्गाप्रीत्यर्थं सप्तश्लोकी दुर्गापाठे विनियोगः ॥

Om asya
śrīdurgāsaptaślokīstotramahāmantrasya
nārāyaṇa ṛṣiḥ
anuṣṭubhādīni chandāṃsi
śrīmahākālīmahālakṣmīmahāsarasvatyo
devatāḥ

śrīdūrgāprītyarthaṃ saptaślokī durgāpāṭhe
viniyogaḥ

For the great mantra of durgaa saptashlokee lord Naaraayana is the seer (rishi)

The meters used in the hymn is anushtup and other

The goddesses praised through this hymn are Mahaakaalee, Mahaalakshmee and Mahaasarasvatee

This hymn is chanted for the purpose of pleasing mother Durgaa.

Shloka 1

ज्ञानिनामपि चेतांसि देवी भगवती हि सा ।
बलादाकृष्य मोहाय महामाया प्रयच्छति ॥१॥

jñāninām api cetāṃsi devī bhagavatī hi sā |
balādākṛṣya mohāya mahāmāyā prayacchati
||1||

This shloka is from the first chapter of Devi Maahaatmyam. This shloka is said by the sage Sumedhas to the king Surata and Samaadhi the trader, glorifying the greatness of the goddess.

This shloka addresses the goddess with three names.

Devi - we already discussed the meaning of Devi in the poorva peetikaa.

Bhagavatee - One who has the six godly qualities.

ऐश्वर्यस्य समग्रस्य धर्मस्य यशस: श्रिय:
ज्ञानवैराग्ययोश्चैव षण्णां भाग इतीरिणा

aiśvaryasya samagrasya dharmasya yaśasa: śriyah
jñānavairāgyayōścaiva ṣaṇṇāṃ bhāga itīriṇā

Complete lordship, complete righteousness, limitless glory, limitless wealth, skills, Complete wisdom and detachment. These are the six great qualities called Bhaga and its completeness is found only in almighty god and his power (Shakti) who is non-different to him.

Demigods, humans and others may also have these qualities but with their own limits and defects. These qualities are only shown in its completeness in almighty gods and the forms taken by them to save the world and bless the devotees.

Mahaamaayaa - The power of the almighty Brahman. Maayaa is the might of the almighty. The capability of doing the five great deeds (creation, protection, destruction, disappearance and blessing) The power which overpowers everything and every rules of possibility. The lord can do anything and everything through this power and mother goddess is the embodiment of this power which has taken the form of the mistress of Brahman.

The Shvetaashvatara Upanishad says about the Mahaamaayaa who is also the Paraashakti - the great power of the Brahman as such

परास्य शक्तिर्विविधैव श्रूयते
स्वाभाविकी ज्ञानबलक्रिया च
parāsya śaktirvividhaiva śrūyate
svābhāvikī jñānabalakriyā ca

His greatest power is stated in many different forms, his wisdom, might and actions which are naturally possessed by him.

Mahaamaayaa is the source from which three gunas are born (satva, rajas and tamas) and she is the controller of three gunas, the entire universe is made out of three gunas and hence she is the controller of the entire universe.

The Shaastras say that the Brahman (ABSOLUTE GOD) doesn't do anything directly. All that which are done are done through his ultimate power. That power is none other than our beloved mother goddess Shakti. She is known by different names and in different forms.

In this shloka, a strong example of her power and capability is given.

The Devi Bhagavati can forcibly attract the minds of even the wise (Gyaanis) and give their minds completely to delusion. (i.e.) she can put even their minds in complete control of delusion.

Here the word Gyaani doesn't mean a self realized soul (Jeevanmukta) but a wise person who has attained wisdom through his study. Though the person has studied that everything and everyone is purely Brahman alone and nothing other than Brahman exists, he falls in the delusion of separation and false imagery of the sense of manyness because of the different names and forms which are nothing but

Brahman.

Though he has studied that names and forms are just reflections (false images) of Brahman and nothing else really exists, he still acts according the mind's false ideas. That is pointed out in this shloka.

But why does our kind mother do that? We should understand that the world runs only due to this false imagery of separation from Brahman. Even a wise man has destined deeds which are to be completed by him in the world and till he has those karma (both good and bad) to be experienced, he cannot enjoy the true wisdom of self realization and hence the mother puts his mind in delusions.

Only because of the false feeling of manyness, the man does good to others, teach others, share knowledge, help the needy etc. A self realized soul sees and experiences everything as Brahman. A Jeevanmukta cannot dive into action neither good nor bad. He has nothing left to do as he doesn't have the ego or doership. Sometimes mother goddess puts one's mind temporarily in to delusion for the sake of the welfare of the world.

For example a realized soul (Jeevanmukta) can implant his wisdom to a disciple only if he sees that the disciple is having a problem in understanding the eternal truth. If the Jeevanmukta sees the disciple as absolute god who is the all knower, why would he even think of implanting wisdom. Though the guru knows that everything is Brahman, the disciple is also Brahman, the guru sees ignorance in the disciple only because of Mahaamaayaa's grace of putting him in to mild delusion. Because there is no actual ignorance in Brahman, like there is no darkness in the presence of sun.

By worshipping mother in this form we will get a thought "O mother! When you can put great Gyaanis and gurus in delusion, then what about me? O Devi! Please pity me and save me from ignorance and bless me with true wisdom."

By worshipping so, we are slowly freed from all delusions by our kind mother goddess.

Every shloka of Durgaa saptashloki is also a mantra that can be chanted separately to please mother Durgaa and attain various fruits.

This mantra can be chanted for 108 times or 1000 times or 10000 times daily for gaining self-control, control over senses and gaining control over others.

Shloka 2

दुर्गे स्मृता हरसि भीतिमशेषजन्तोः
स्वस्थैः स्मृता मतिमतीव शुभां ददासि ।
दारिद्र्यदुःखभयहारिणि का त्वदन्या
सर्वोपकारकरणाय सदाऽऽर्द्रचित्ता ॥ २॥

durge smṛtā harasi bhītimaśeṣajantoḥ
svasthaiḥ smṛtā matimatīva śubhāṃ dadāsi ।
dāridryaduḥkhabhayahāriṇi kā tvadanyā
sarvopakārakaraṇāya sadā"rdracittā ॥ 2 ॥

This is the sixteenth shloka from the chapter four of Devi Maahaatmyam. This is sung by the Devas (demigods) in praise of the goddess.

This shloka addresses the goddess by the name Durgaa and praises the her glory and the glory of her name.

The word 'Durga' means difficulty or situations which are very hard to go through and cross over. Troubles that can't be easily solved are called Durga.

One who makes such situations easy for us and helps us cross over them is called Durgaa.

The shloka uses the word Durge with two meanings.

Durge smrutaa means when you are remembered in times of trouble and situations which are never ending and hard to pass through ....

Durge smruta also means O goddess Durgaa,

when you are remembered ....

That way the shloka praises the glory of the goddess and also her sacred name.

The name Durgaa is praised even in the Vedas in mantra two of Durgaa sookta

तामग्निवर्णां तपसा ज्वलन्तीं वैरोचनीं कर्मफलेषु जुष्टाम्
दुर्गां देवीँशरणमहं प्रपद्ये सुतरसि तरसे नमः

tāmagnivarṇāṃ tapasā jvalantīṃ vairocanīṃ karmaphaleṣu juṣṭām
durgāṃ devīँśaraṇamahaṃ prapadye sutarasi tarase namaḥ

Also in Devi Upanishad

तामग्निवर्णां तपसा ज्वलन्तीं वैरोचनीं कर्मफलेषु जुष्टाम्
दुर्गां देवीं शरणमहं प्रपद्ये सुतरां नाशयते तमः

tāmagnivarṇāṃ tapasā jvalantīṃ vairocanīṃ karmaphaleṣu juṣṭām
durgāṃ devīṃ śaraṇamahaṃ prapadye sutarāṃ nāśayate tamaḥ

In Mundamaalaa Tantra the meaning of the word Durgaa is given as such

दुर्गो दैत्ये महाविघ्ने भवबन्धे कुकर्मणि
शोके दुखे च नरके यमदण्डे च जन्मनि

महाभये च रोगे चाप्याशब्दो हन्तृवाचक:
एतान्हन्त्येव या देवी सा दुर्गा परिकीर्तिता

durgo daitye mahāvighne bhavabandhe kukarmaṇi
śoke dukhe ca narake yamadaṇḍe ca janmani
mahābhaye ca roge cāpyāśabdo hantṛvācaka:
etānhantyeva yā devī sā durgā parikīrtitā

The word 'durga' refers to demon, big obstacles and hindrances, bondage of worldliness (samsaara), bad deeds, sorrow, pain, hell, punishment of Yama (the god of death), birth, great fears, diseases.

Ā means destroyer

Durgaa means destroyer of all kinds of durga. She protects us from demons and negative forces, she liberates us by blessing us with self realization, she guides us in the path of right deeds and stops us from indulging in bad deeds, she rectifies our sorrow and heals our pain. She saves us from hell (Naraka) and punishments of Yama by purifying us from our sins and guiding us in the right path. She cures all our diseases which are the outcome of our past sins.

This shloka praises the above qualities of Durgaa.

durge smṛtā harasi bhītimaśeṣajantoḥ

When you are remembered in the times of hardship and troubles, you rectify them completely. You also remove our fears from everything.

Our mother goddess loves us and when we (her children) call her in mind, think of her, she rescues us immediately from all troubles and rectifies all our fears out of her unconditional love for us.

svasthaiḥ smṛtā matimatīva śubhāṃ dadāsi ।

In previous line of the shloka, we have learnt how she rescues us instantaneously as we think of her and now that we thought of her and after she rescues us from troubles and fear, we are free, fine and peaceful. Now what will she give us when we think of her?

Now that we are saved from troubles, why would we think of her? Of course we would think of her. Now that we are saved from all troubles, we have experienced her power and greatness. It is natural for us to remember her with love and gratitude. Now that we have no troubles or problems, what will she do for us when we remember her? It is the nature of our mother goddess to do some kind of good to us whenever she is remembered, called and prayed.

That is described in this line of the shloka.

When remembered by the ones who are fine and peaceful, you bless them with very pure and clear mind and thought.

By doing so she protects us from the troubles we may get into in the future. (i.e.) when we have clear state of mind, the chances of getting into or facing troubles are very less and when we are pure minded we won't indulge in bad deeds or sins. As sins are the cause of all sorrow, we won't be experiencing sorrow or bad times since we have no sins now.

From this verse, we understand that we should always do remembrance of her and her holy name so that we are always pure.

Now the third line glorifies the goddesses' kindness

dāridryaduḥkhabhayahāriṇi kā tvadanyā

Who else would destroy poverty, sorrow and fear like you.

Here you may get a doubt. Wouldn't other gods also rectify these?

We know that all the gods are the form of the

same Brahman. Be it Shiva, Vishnu, Surya, or Ganapati then what could be the meaning of this verse?

Though all the gods and goddesses are the form of the Brahman (absolute god) Durgaa is the mother goddess and she has the incomparable love and kindness and she is our best protector as she is our mother.

This incomparable love for us beings is explained further in the next line of the shloka.

sarvopakārakaraṇāya sadā''rdracittā

You are the one who is always kind and you are happily ready to help us all.

Mantra Shaastras say that by chanting this shloka daily, regularly for thousand and eight times or hundred and eight times, you get mother's protection from fears, troubles, diseases, poverty etc.

Shloka 3

सर्वमङ्गलमाङ्गल्ये शिवे सर्वार्थसाधिके ।
शरण्ये त्र्यम्बके गौरि नारायणि नमोऽस्तु ते ॥ ३॥

sarvamaṅgalamāṅgalye śive sarvārthasādhike ।
śaraṇye tryambake gauri nārāyaṇi namo'stu te ॥
3॥

This is the ninth shloka from chapter eleven of Devi Maahaatmyam.

Sarvamangalamaangalye - The word mangala means auspicious, prosperous, lucky etc. maangalye means one who is the auspiciousness present in all that is auspicious and the prosperity in all that is prosperous. (i.e.) The mother goddess is auspicious than all that which is auspicious. The greatest auspicious. One who is the greatest level of prosperity and luck. One who is the giver of luck for all the lucky and one who has blessed prosperity for all who prosper. She is the quality of auspiciousness and prosperity. So if we worship her, we will also be fortunate and prosperous.

Mangala also means good. The one who does auspicious and good deeds. Maangalye means one who is good and thinks of the welfare of.

By this sarvamangalamaangalye means One who is the reason of welfare of all those who are good and the doers of auspicious deeds. Sarvamangalamaangalye means One who cares for the welfare of the good.

Shive- The word Shivaa means one who is gracious, auspicious, embodiment of bliss, kind, benignant.

The word shivaa is a Synonym of the words bhadraa and svasherayasee

bhadraa means she who is good, pleasant, great

svashreyas means ultimate welfare. (liberation)

Shivaa means she who has great qualities like sarvagyathva - all knowing capacity sarvyashaktitva - almightiness etc.

Shivaa means the completely pure.

She is also called Shivaa for she is the consort of lord Shiva. The word Shivaa is the feminine gender word which has all the meanings of the masculine gender word Shiva (i.e.) Shivaa (goddess Gauri) has all the qualities of lord Shiva. Shiva and Shakti are one and they just took different forms to bless their devotees. Shiva and Shakti cannot be separated.

In Devi puraana the meaning of name shivaa is explained in the below shloka.

शिवा मुक्तिः समाख्याता तत्प्रदत्वात् शिवा स्मृता
śivā mukti: samākhyātā tatpradatvāt śivā smṛtā

Shivaa means Mukti (liberation) and one who blesses us with liberation is called shivaa.

Sarvaarthasaadhike - One who helps us attain all kinds of purushaarthaas (dharma - righteousness, artha - wealth kaama - desires and moksha -liberation.)

धर्मादींश्चिन्तिता यस्मात् सर्वलोकस्य यच्छति
अतो देवी समाख्याता लोके सर्वार्थसाधिका

dharmādīṃścintitā yasmāt sarvalokasya yacchati
ato devī samākhyātā loke sarvārthasādhikā

When done remembrance of her, she gives all the purushaarthaas (attainments of life) and hence she is known as sarvaartha saadhikaa.

sharanye - One who is to be sought refuge from. The best protector of the surrendered.

In Devi Puraana, the meaning of this name is explained by the below shloka.

विषाग्निभयघोरेषु शरण्यास्मरणाद्यत:
शरण्या तेन सा देवी मुनिभि: परिकीर्तिता

viṣāgnibhayaghoreṣu śaraṇyāsmaraṇādyata:
śaraṇyā tena sā devī munibhi: parikīrtitā

She is the shelter (protection) from poisons, fire, fears and other terrible troubles and hence she is called Sharanyaa by the great Rishis. (seers)

Mother when remembered with devotion protects us from everything and is our best protector and shelter. She takes us in shelter immediately when we surrender to her as she is our loving mother.

tryambake - tri means three, ambaka means eye, tryambakaa means one who has three eyes.

The shloka explaining the meaning of tryambakaa is given in devi puraana

सोमसूर्यानालाक्षित्वात् त्र्यंबका सा स्मृता बुधै:
somasūryānālākṣitvāt tryaṃbakā sā smṛtā budhai:

she is called Tryambakaa for she has moon, sun and fire as her eyes.

Gauri - she who is pure white in color. The while color is the symbol of purity.

Naaraayani - naara - group of beings. ayana - shelter. Naaraayani means she who is the shelter of all beings. She is non-different to Naaraayana so she is called Naaraayani. She is the Yogamaayaa who is non-different to

Naaraayana.

The oneness of Devi and Naaraayana is also stated in the Upanishads.

या उमा सा स्वयं विष्णु: - रुद्रहृदयोपनिशत्
yā umā sā svayaṃ viṣṇu: - rudrahrudayōpaniṡat

Lord Vishnu is none other than goddess Umaa the Shakti and eternal consort of Shiva.

She who is the power of Naaraayana in the form of goddess Mahaalakshmi.

namostu - let there be salutations/ hails

te - to you /for you

By chanting the shloka seven times daily, one gets blessed with various benefits and luck.

This mantra can be chanted for the fulfillment of desires for 108 times or 1000 times or 10000 times daily.

Shloka 4

शरणागतदीनार्तपरित्राणपरायणे ।
सर्वस्यार्तिहरे देवि नारायणि नमोऽस्तु ते ॥ ४॥

śaraṇāgatadīnārta paritrāṇaparāyaṇe ।
sarvasyārtihare devi nārāyaṇi namo'stu te ॥ 4 ॥

This is the eleventh shloka from chapter eleven of Devi Maahaatmyam. The kindness of the mother is praised in this shloka.

sharanaagatadeenaartaparitraaNa paraayaNe -

O mother! you are the complete protector of Deenas and Aartaas and doing so is your primary aim.

sharanaagata - one who seeks refuge

deena - poor, pitiable, one who is in deep misery, scanty, helpless, one who is suffering from scarcity, timid, sad, depressed, unlucky, wretched

Aarta - afflicted, distressed, unhappy, pained, sick, struck by calamity, injured, struck by calamity, oppressed, troubled, affected by misfortune, disturbed

paritraana - The deed of fully protecting someone, giving complete protection.

Paraayane - One who has a chief objective of or final aim of sarvasyaartihare - Rectifier of everyone's Aarti. She being our beloved mother, rectifies all our Aarti. (she is the mother of all the worlds and hence the word sarvaysa is used.)

sarvasya - of everyone

aartihare - She who completely removes (rectifies) Aarti. Aarti is the feeling of an Aarta. I have already explained you who an Aarta is. Mother completely removes the Aarti of an Aarta. (i.e.) she rectifies all the reasons for the aarti and makes happy.

Devi - the meaning of the name Devi has already been explained. The word Devi is used here in the meaning playful (i.e.) capable of doing anything and everything effortlessly and hence she is also capable of rectifying all our pains and sorrows effortlessly.

Naaraayani - In this shloka this name is used to refer Devi because Naaraayani means shelter of every being and hence she is capable of and is willing to rectify all the Aarti because it is her nature.

namostu te - salutations to you

The inner meaning which the shloka expresses is O mother, you are the complete protector of everyone and everything and you are the ultimate shelter to all beings. You protect all the worlds and rectify the sorrow and pain of everyone and then when we come in refuge to you it is obvious that you will protect us and save us definitely. You protect the worlds without being asked for protection from all the beings living in it, so we trust you will definitely protect us when we particularly request your protection and surrender to you.

You have protecting us completely as your primary objective and aim. Hence we have no doubt in whether or not we will get protection from you.

This mantra can be chanted for 108 times or 1000 times or 10000 times daily for the purpose of protection from diseases and rectification of diseases, disaster, pain and calamity.

Shloka 5

सर्वस्वरूपे सर्वेशे सर्वशक्तिसमन्विते ।
भयेभ्यस्त्राहि नो देवि दुर्गे देवि नमोऽस्तु ते ॥ ५॥

sarvasvarūpe sarveśe sarvaśaktisamanvite ।
bhayebhyastrāhi no devi durge devi namo'stu te॥
5॥

This is the twenty third shloka from chapter eleven of Devi Maahaatmyam. In this shloka the different qualities and attributes of goddess Durgaa are praised.

sarvasvaroope - O One who is in the form of everything. One who is omnipresent, one whose form is this entire world.

sarveshe - O one who owns everything and everyone.

Sarva means everyone and everything

ईश ऐश्वर्ये
īśa aiśvaryē

Aishwarya means wealth, power, supremacy, prosperity, might, sovereignty, godhood, domination, controllership, sway.

She who has all these qualities or any of these qualities is called Eeshaa.

Eeshaa means lord, leader, greatest

Sarveshaa means she who owns everything. (i.e.) her ownership and controllership has no limits. She is also greater than everything and everyone else.

We can see descriptions of Vishnu, Indra, Varuna, Soma, Agni and other gods worshipping goddess Durgaa in the Puraanas.

sarvashaktisamanvite- All powerful. Her power is limitless, she is capable of doing anything and everything she wants to. The word Shaktisamanvite can be taken for two meanings, one that she has different kinds of great powers of doing different deeds. Two. She is accompanied with different Shaktis - feminine goddesses who is her amshas (partial forms) like Braamhi, Maaheshwari, Vaishnavi, etc and zillions of Shakti gaNaas.

bhayebhya: traahi nah - Save us from all fears. The prayer to save us from fears also implicitly is a prayer to destroy the reasons of fear like poverty, disease and enemies (internal and external).

Devi - The meaning of the name Devi has already been explained. Here the name Devi is used to express that she is bright and luminous even while rescuing us from troubles, she has a pure smile in her face.

Durge Devi - The meaning of the name Durgaa has already been explained in shloka two. The word Devi is used here to indicate that her act of saving is effortless and playful. She doesn't get tired saving us.

The word Devi is repeated twice in the shloka out of great respect to the goddess and her glory and greatness.

namostu te - salutations to you

This mantra can be chanted for 108 times or 1000 times or 10000 times daily for the purpose of protection and getting out of fears.

Shloka 6

रोगानशेषानपहंसि तुष्टा रुष्टा तु कामान् सकलानभीष्टान् ।
त्वामाश्रितानां न विपन्नराणां त्वामाश्रिताह्याश्रयतां प्रयान्ति
॥ ६॥

rogānaśeṣānapahaṃsi tuṣṭā
ruṣṭā tu kāmān sakalānabhīṣṭān ।
tvāmāśritānāṃ na vipannarāṇāṃ
tvāmāśrithyāśrayatāṃ prayānti ॥ 6 ॥

This is the twenty eighth shloka from chapter eleven of Devi Maahaathmyam.

rogaanasheshaanapahamsi thustaa - When you are pleased by us, you destroy all our diseases and troubles. When is the mother goddess pleased? She is pleased when we are good and righteous. When we do good deeds and be honest, walk in the path of dharma (righteousness) and when we follow the values and morals we were taught by her (i.e.) living in the way of life instructed by the Vedas, Smrutis and Puraanas. If we are not able to live righteously but we want to live so wholeheartedly and we pray to her. She purifies us and leads us in the path of righteousness.

Here the word Roga which literally means disease also indicates other problems which sicken us. That is if we be righteous and worship goddess Durgaa with true devotion, she rectifies all the problems which affects us.

rushtaa tu kaamaan sakalaanabheeshtaan - When you are angry on us, you destroy all our desires (i.e.) you stop us from attaining our desires. Mother gets angry when we are not righteous and good. She punishes us to correct us and make us lead a righteous life. She destroys all our desires and makes us repent for our mistakes but we should always remember that when we realize our faults and seek forgiveness truly, she forgives us and helps us become good by purifying us and blessing us with a pure mind. She does this because she loves us even when she punishes us. Her punishments are not out of hatred for us but out of care and love for us.

tvaamaashritaanaam na vipannaraanaam -

tvaam - to you.

aashritaanaam - those who have sought refuge

naraanaam- for the humans (beings)

vipat - misfortune, accident, ruin, trouble, danger, failure, calamity, perishing

na - no

Those who have sought refuge from you by worshipping you wholeheartedly and surrendering to you don't have any vipat. (i.e.) you stop all kinds of troubles from reaching them even before they know it or even when some troubles reach them, you protect them from being troubled by it and make them feel that they are not in trouble at all. meaning every hard situation passes easily.

tvaamaashritaa hi aashrayataam prayaanti -

tvaamaashritaa - one who has sought refuge from you.

hi - only

aashrayataam - the quality to be sought refuge from.

prayaanti - gets in to a particular state on condition attains the status of.

The true devotees of the mother goddess are not only protected from troubles but also blessed with the greatness and power of giving protection to the ones who seek refuge from them.

This mantra can be chanted for 108 times or 1000 times or 10000 times daily for the purpose of protection from diseases and complete cure of diseases.

Shloka 7

सर्वाबाधाप्रशमनं त्रैलोक्यस्याखिलेश्वरि ।
एवमेव त्वया कार्यमस्मद्वैरि विनाशनम् ॥ ७॥

sarvābādhāpraśamanaṃ trailokyasyākhileśvari I
evameva tvayā kāryamasmadvairi vināśanam II
7 II

This is the thirty ninth shloka from chapter eleven of Devi Maahaathmyam.

In this shloka goddess is addressed by the name Akhileshwari.

Sarva- every, all

Aa - the prefix aa is given to the word baadhaa in this shloka. The prefix Aa means complete and continuous.

baadhaa - suffering, pain, injury, obstacle, hardship, trouble, danger, one that which hurts or affects negatively

aabaadhaa means continuous baadhaa.

Pra - the prefix means well, nicely

shamanam - pacification of, curing, healing, destroying, killing

sarva aabaadhaa prashamanam means the complete prasharamana of all baadhaa. The meaning of the words prashanamana and baadhaa are given above.

Trailokyasya - of all the three worlds (earth, space and underworld).

Akhileshwaree - O owner and controller of the worlds.

Evam eva - only like this.

Tvayaa - by you

Kaaryam - should be done.

Asmad - our

Vairi - enemy, foe

Vinaashanam - complete destruction of

The meaning of the shloka is O Akhileshwari! The destruction of our foes should be done by you such that the pacification and destruction of all kinds of suffering and pain of all the worlds happen.

The word evam eva has great importance in this shloka. The word is used to express that you should destroy our enemies only in such a way that all the sufferings of the worlds end.

Here the enemy means the problems troubling all the worlds and by destroying the cause of the problems, the world should gain peace and liberty from sufferings and pain. This is prayed to the goddess because she is Akhileshwaree - the owner and controller of the worlds, she is the ruler of the worlds and hence she should protect and maintain peace in the worlds.

Here the prayer also indicates that the enemy of the worlds is the enemy to everyone residing in it. Through this shloka, mother goddess is requested to destroy all negative forces which are disturbing the world and killing it's peace.

The part asmad vairi vinaashanam - destruction of my enemy also means the destruction of your bad thoughts and actions which harm you and the worlds, the environment and the ecology.

This shloka can also be explained as O mother you are the owner of the world, hence you are the one to destroy the pains and sufferings of the worlds and I am also owned by you (as I am also a part of this world.) and hence O mother please kill my sufferings and enemies as it is your nature to pacify sufferings and enemies and protect your people (your children - all the beings of the world.)

I pray this to you because you are capable of

protecting everything in this world and please do protect me also, freeing me from all the pains, sufferings and enemies.

This shloka is also used to pray the goddess for pacifying our enemy who is really bad or evil and when we are honest and righteous Mother always supports us.

This mantra can be chanted for 108 times or 1000 times or 10000 times daily for the destruction of all troubles, suffering and pain.

Durgaa Saptashlokee in Devanagari Script

सप्तश्लोकी दुर्गा

शिव उवाच
देवि त्वं भक्तसुलभे सर्वकार्यविधायिनी ।
कलौ हि कार्यसिद्ध्यर्थमुपायं ब्रूहि यत्नतः ॥

देव्युवाच
शृणु देव प्रवक्ष्यामि कलौ सर्वेष्टसाधनम् ।
मया तवैव स्नेहेनाप्यम्बास्तुतिः प्रकाश्यते ॥

ॐ अस्य श्रीदुर्गासप्तश्लोकीस्तोत्रमहामन्त्रस्य
नारायण ऋषिः ।
अनुष्टुभादीनि छन्दांसि ।
श्रीमहाकालीमहालक्ष्मीमहासरस्वत्यो देवताः ।
श्रीदूर्गाप्रीत्यर्थं सप्तश्लोकी दुर्गापाठे विनियोगः ॥

ज्ञानिनामपि चेतांसि देवी भगवती हि सा ।
बलादाकृष्य मोहाय महामाया प्रयच्छति ॥ १॥

दुर्गे स्मृता हरसि भीतिमशेषजन्तोः
स्वस्थैः स्मृता मतिमतीव शुभां ददासि ।
दारिद्र्यदुःखभयहारिणि का त्वदन्या
सर्वोपकारकरणाय सदाऽऽर्द्रचित्ता ॥ २॥

सर्वमङ्गलमाङ्गल्ये शिवे सर्वार्थसाधिके ।
शरण्ये त्र्यम्बके गौरि नारायणि नमोऽस्तु ते ॥ ३॥

शरणागतदीनार्तपरित्राणपरायणे ।
सर्वस्यार्तिहरे देवि नारायणि नमोऽस्तु ते ॥ ४॥

सर्वस्वरूपे सर्वेशे सर्वशक्तिसमन्विते ।
भयेभ्यस्त्राहि नो देवि दुर्गे देवि नमोऽस्तु ते ॥ ५॥

रोगानशेषानपहंसि तुष्टा
रुष्टा तु कामान् सकलानभीष्टान् ।
त्वामाश्रितानां न विपन्नराणां
त्वामाश्रिता ह्याश्रयतां प्रयान्ति ॥ ६॥

सर्वाबाधाप्रशमनं त्रैलोक्यस्याखिलेश्वरि ।
एवमेव त्वया कार्यमस्मद्वैरि विनाशनम् ॥ ७॥

Durgaa Saptashlokee in english Script

saptaślokī durgā

śiva uvāca
devi tvaṃ bhaktasulabhe sarvakāryavidhāyinī
kalau hi kāryasiddhyarthamupāyaṃ brūhi yatnataḥ

devyuvāca
śṛṇu deva pravakṣyāmi kalau sarveṣṭasādhanam
mayā tavaiva snehenāpyambāstutiḥ prakāśyate

Om asya
śrīdurgāsaptaślokīstotramahāmantrasya
nārāyaṇa ṛṣiḥ
anuṣṭubhādīni chandāṃsi
śrīmahākālīmahālakṣmīmahāsarasvatyo
devatāḥ
śrīdūrgāprītyarthaṃ saptaślokī durgāpāṭhe
viniyogaḥ

jñāninnāmapi cetāṃsi devī bhagavatī hi sā
balādākṛṣya mohāya mahāmāyā prayacchati

durge smṛtā harasi bhītimaśeṣajantoḥ
svasthaiḥ smṛtā matimatīva śubhāṃ dadāsi
dāridryaduḥkhabhayahāriṇi kā tvadanyā
sarvopakārakaraṇāya sadā"rdracittā

sarvamaṅgalamāṅgalye śive sarvārthasādhike
śaraṇye tryambake gauri nārāyaṇi namo'stu te

śaraṇāgatadīnārtaparitrāṇaparāyaṇe
sarvasyārtihare devi nārāyaṇi namo'stu te

sarvasvarūpe sarveśe sarvaśaktisamanvite
bhayebhyastrāhi no devi durge devi namo'stu te

rogānaśeṣānapahaṃsi tuṣṭā
ruṣṭā tu kāmān sakalānabhīṣṭān
tvāmāśritānāṃ na vipannarāṇāṃ
tvāmāśritā hyāśrayatāṃ prayānti

sarvābādhāpraśamanaṃ trailokyasyākhileśvari
evameva tvayā kāryamasmadvairi vināśanam

Contact Me:

You can always feel free to contact me or send me suggestions, doubts to writetokoushik@yahoo.com

Please Leave a Review

Thank you for reading the book. Hope you enjoyed it.

If you like this book and enjoyed reading, it would be really helpful if you can share your experience by **leaving a review**

If you have had any problems with the book, please feel free to message me through email writetokoushik@yahoo.com

I will try my best to help you with it.

Thank you

K.koushik

Other Books by Author

Tales of Hanuman

Tales of Hanuman vol 2

Hanuman Chalisa Explained

The Heart of Sun God - A Hymn from Valmiki Ramayana

19 PLUS TIPS FOR USING GMAIL TO THE FULLEST

Who Should Start a Membership Business

Glories of Shiva: Kaalahastheeshwara (coming soon)

Glories of Shiva: Stories from the Shiva Mahimna Stotra (coming soon)

All books that are published are available through Amazon.com

Made in United States
Orlando, FL
11 February 2022

14712223R00036